THE FENG SHUI LOVE JOURNAL

A Guided Workbook to Attract Love and Romance into Your Life

THE FENG SHUI
LOVE JOURNAL

A Guided Workbook to Attract Love and Romance into Your Life

THE FENG SHUI LOVE JOURNAL

Published by Complete Feng Shui
Mb: 0421 116 799,
Email: michele@completefengshui.com
Website: www.completefengshui.com

The Feng Shui Love Journal©
Text copyright © Michele Castle
Illustrations copyright © Michele Castle

All rights reserved, no part of this publication may be reproduced, stored in a retrieval system or transmitted, in any form, or by any means, electronic, mechanical, photocopying, recording, or otherwise, without the prior written permission from Complete Feng Shui.

The moral right of the author to be identified as the author of this book has been asserted. Author: Michele Castle
Design copyright@completefengshui Title: The Feng Shui Love Journal Journal

This Journal has been written to offer tips, symbolism insight and planning with Feng Shui principals. The author editor and publisher take no responsibility for the outcome of any information implemented from this journal.

ISBN: 978-0-6459620-8-6 (Paperback)
ISBN: 978-0-6459620-9-3 (Hardcover)
ISBN: 978-0-6459620-2-4 (Spiral Bound)

Platinum member of the Association of Feng Shui Consultants (AFSC)
Recognised Feng Shui training institution by the (AFSC)

 facebook@completefengshui   instagram@completefengshui

Book Cover, Book Layout & eBook Conversion by manuscript2ebook.com

CONTENTS

Welcome	7
Introduction	9
About the Author	11
Journalling	12
Exercise 1 Reflection on Self-Love	20
Exercise 2 Decluttering to Create Space	30
Exercise 3 Identifying Relationship Patterns	40
Exercise 4 Enhancing Communications	50
Exercise 5 Balancing Giving and Receiving	60
Exercise 6 Releasing Past Hurts	70
Exercise 7 Creating a Love Vision Board	80
Exercise 8 Strengthening Trust	90
Exercise 9 Honouring Intimacy and Vulnerability	100
Exercise 10 Clearing Emotional and Physical Space	110
Exercise 11 Setting Relationship Goals	120
Exercise 12 Embracing Gratitude	130
Exercise 13 Cultivating Self-Compassion	140
Exercise 14 Visualising Abundance in Love	150
Exercise 15 Embodying Confidence in Love	160
Self-Love Journey Checklist	164
About the Author	166

Welcome to the incredible world of Journaling! Journaling can help in the management of personal adversity and can change and emphasise *important* patterns and growth in life. Writing your thoughts, feelings, and actions down in a journal allows you to connect to your values, emotions, and goals, enabling you to craft and maintain a sense of self. It can help you reflect on your experiences and discover your authentic self.

Scientifically, journaling can help you:

1. Achieve goals
2. Track progress and growth
3. Gain self-confidence
4. Improve writing and communication skills
5. Reduce stress and anxiety
6. Find inspiration
7. Strengthen memory
8. Add the benefit of everyday Feng Shui tips and watch your life truly evolve…

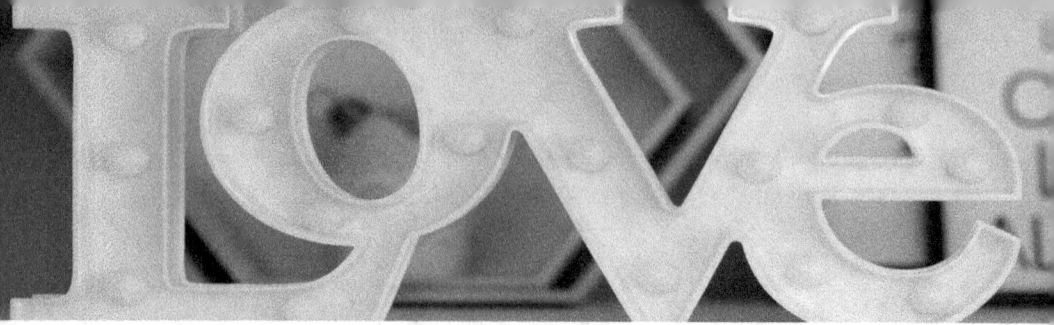

Thank you for choosing to embark on this journey of self-discovery, growth, and love with the Love and Relationship Self-Help Journal. It has been a true honour to guide you through these reflections and exercises. I hope they have brought clarity, healing, and a deeper understanding of yourself and your relationships.

I wish that the insights and tools you've gained through this journal continue to enrich your life and guide you toward the love and connection you deserve. Remember, love is an ongoing journey, and practising self-awareness, mindfulness, and feng shui can continue to deepen your relationships over time. These are powerful tools that can empower you and put you in control of your personal growth and relationships.

I encourage you to keep applying feng shui principles to create balance, harmony, and positive energy in all areas of your life. For instance, you can arrange your living space to promote relaxation and communication, or use colors and elements that resonate with your personal energy. Your home is a powerful reflection of your inner world; by nurturing it, you also nurture your heart.

As you continue on this self-growth path, I invite you to explore the fascinating world of Chinese astrology. Understanding your Chinese zodiac sign and the energies influencing your life can open up even more possibilities for self-discovery and personal alignment. It can help you know your strengths and challenges and how they affect your relationships. Both feng shui and Chinese astrology offer wisdom that can help you live with intention, harmony, and fulfilment.

Thank you for trusting me to be part of your journey. Your trust is deeply appreciated, and I am sending you love, light, and all the positive energy for the next chapter of your life.

With love and gratitude,

Michele

INTRODUCTION: WHY USE THIS JOURNAL?

Relationships are one of the most significant aspects of our lives, offering us joy, connection, and growth, but they also come with challenges that require patience, self-awareness, and effort. Whether you are in a relationship, seeking one, or focusing on self-love, it's essential to cultivate a deep connection with both yourself and your environment to experience the fullness of love.

This journal is designed to be a personal tool that helps you reflect on the many layers of love, from how you give and receive it to how you can enhance it through mindful practices. Rooted in the principles of feng shui, a Chinese philosophical system of harmonizing everyone with the surrounding environment, self-discovery, and personal growth, it offers you space to explore your patterns, heal past wounds, and align your emotional and physical environment with your intentions for love and connection.

Using this journal, you are embarking on a transformative journey. The prompts and exercises will guide you to look inward, ask meaningful questions, and take actionable steps to enhance the love you experience in your relationships and home. Think of it as a map, helping you uncover what's needed to cultivate a more fulfilling love life while creating an environment that energetically supports your goals.

This is more than just a journal; it's a space for profound personal growth, healing, and renewal. Through the exercises, you'll develop greater clarity, deepen your understanding of love, and make meaningful shifts in your inner and outer worlds. By the end of this journey, you'll be equipped with the self-awareness, tools, and feng shui principles to invite more profound, more harmonious relationships into your life. Let this journal be your guide, offering daily insights and practices to help you foster the love and connection you desire.

ABOUT THE AUTHOR AND THE CREATION OF THIS JOURNAL

Michele Castle is an internationally recognised feng shui expert, life coach, and transformational speaker. Her unique approach, blending the principles of feng shui with personal development, is a testament to her passion for helping individuals align their lives and environments to create harmonious, love-filled relationships. With years of experience in holistic healing and a profound understanding of the emotional and spiritual journey of love, Michele has guided countless people toward greater self-awareness, balance, and emotional fulfilment.

The **Love and Relationship Self-Help Journal** is more than just a book. It's a personal companion, created for anyone seeking to deepen their understanding of love, improve their relationships, and align their home with the energy of romance and harmony. This journal, infused with Michele's expertise in feng shui and her profound understanding of the emotional and spiritual journey of love, is designed to be by your side as you cultivate a loving relationship with yourself, your partner, and your environment.

Whether you're looking to attract new love, nurture an existing relationship, or connect more deeply with your heart, this journal is your guide. It offers a structured path to self-reflection, healing, and growth, using the wisdom of feng shui and mindful self-exploration. Michele invites you to embark on this journey, opening your heart and home to the love you deserve.

True love begins with self-love.

....
....
....
....
....
....
....
....

Communicate openly, even when it's uncomfortable.

....
....
....
....
....
....
....
....

Let go of past hurts to make room for new love.

Healthy boundaries create space for a deeper connection.

....
....
....
....
....
....
....
....
....
....
....
....
....
....

Love is a choice you make every day.

....
....
....
....
....
....
....
....
....
....
....
....
....
....

Be the partner you wish to have.

Forgiveness is a gift you give yourself.

Vulnerability is the gateway to intimacy.

Appreciate the small acts of love in your life.

Kindness is the foundation of lasting relationships.

Let your actions speak louder than your words.

Trust is built one small moment at a time.

Give your partner the benefit of the doubt.

Healthy love grows when both partners feel heard.

Release control and trust the flow of love.

True intimacy starts with emotional honesty.

Be patient with your partner's imperfections.

The energy you bring into a relationship is what you receive.

Celebrate your partner's successes as your own.

....
....
....
....
....
....
....
....
....
....
....

Quality time is the secret to nurturing love.

....
....
....
....
....
....
....
....
....
....
....
....

Gratitude turns what you have into enough.

Learn to be comfortable with silence in love.

Love is not about perfection but connection.

Be your partner's safe space under challenging times.

This exercise is designed to promote deeper self-awareness, improve your relationship dynamics, and incorporate feng shui principles that support love and harmony in your home, offer a path to a more fulfilling and harmonious life.

Exercise 1: Reflecting on Self-Love

Question: How do I nurture self-love in my life, and how does it affect my relationships? By reflecting on these questions, you empower yourself to take control of your life and relationships.

Action: Spend 10 minutes journaling about the ways you currently practice self-love. Identify one area where you can improve your self-care. As a feng shui action, enhance the Southwest corner of your home with symbols of self-love, such as a mirror or rose quartz, to reflect your intention of prioritising self-compassion.

Practice empathy, especially when you disagree.

....
....
....
....
....
....
....
....
....

The most robust relationships are built on friendship.

....
....
....
....
....
....
....
....
....

Love grows when you water it daily.

Choose love over fear in every moment.

Listen with the intent to understand, not to reply.

Give without expecting anything in return.

Be the reason your partner feels seen and valued.

Love begins when judgment ends.

Stay curious about your partner's inner world.

Intimacy is about being fully present with each other.

Apologise sincerely when you're wrong.

Release unrealistic expectations and embrace reality.

Healthy love respects individuality.

Celebrate love in its everyday moments, not just on special occasions.

Love is an ever-evolving journey, not a destination.

Laughter is the glue that holds love together.

Your partner is your mirror; love them as you love yourself.

Love requires effort, but it should never feel like a chore.

Be quick to listen and slow to anger.

Cherish the present moments of love; they are fleeting.

Sometimes, love means letting go.

Create space for both togetherness and independence.

Love is felt more in actions than in words.

Honour your partner's emotions as you do your own.

This exercise is designed to promote deeper self-awareness, improve your relationship dynamics, and incorporate feng shui principles that support love and harmony in your home, offer a path to a more fulfilling and harmonious life.

Exercise 2: Decluttering to Create Space for Love. Decluttering is not just about tidying up, it's about making space for love and harmony to enter your life. Are you ready for this transformative change?

Decluttering your home, especially the bedroom or the Southwest corner, is a crucial step in creating a space that invites love and harmony.

Action: Choose one area of your home—especially the bedroom or the Southwest corner—and spend 30 minutes decluttering. Remove items from past relationships or things that no longer serve you. Afterward, place something meaningful to symbolise new beginnings, such as fresh flowers or a love affirmation.

Don't let pride get in the way of love.

The best relationships allow for growth and change.

Trust takes years to build and seconds to break.

Show love through consistency and reliability.

Conflict is natural; how you resolve it matters.

Stay patient with your partner's healing process.

Prioritise love over being right.

Remember, love is a verb.

Celebrate your partner's uniqueness; don't try to change them.

True love stands the test of time and space.

You are responsible for your happiness.

Express love daily through small gestures of affection.

A relationship is a partnership, not ownership.

_____
_____
_____
_____
_____
_____
_____
_____
_____
_____

Self-care is essential to showing up fully in love.

_____
_____
_____
_____
_____
_____
_____
_____
_____
_____

Love yourself first, and others will follow.

Be kind even when it's hard.

Make love a priority, not an afterthought.

Your relationship with yourself sets the tone for all other relationships.

Patience in love brings peace.

....
....
....
....
....
....
....
....
....
....
....

Communicate your needs clearly and kindly.

....
....
....
....
....
....
....
....
....
....
....
....

Be each other's biggest supporters.

In love, small actions create significant impacts.

...

True love grows in an environment of trust and respect.

...

Don't take your partner for granted—express gratitude daily.

This exercise is designed to promote deeper self-awareness, improve your relationship dynamics, and incorporate feng shui principles that support love and harmony in your home, offer a path to a more fulfilling and harmonious life.

Exercise 3: Identifying Relationship Patterns

Identifying and understanding the patterns in your relationships is critical to breaking free from unhealthy cycles and fostering positive change.

Action: Reflect on your past relationships and identify recurring themes. Are there similar issues or behaviours? Write down one positive change you can make to shift these patterns. To support this action with feng shui, introduce a paired object, such as two candles, to symbolise balance and unity in your relationships.

Allow love to flow without trying to control it.

_____
_____
_____
_____
_____
_____
_____
_____
_____
_____

Stay curious about your partner's growth.

_____
_____
_____
_____
_____
_____
_____
_____
_____
_____

Forgive yourself for past mistakes in love.

Love allows space for both joy and sorrow.

Be willing to grow with your partner through life's seasons.

Love is resilient when nurtured.

Let go of old stories that no longer serve your relationship.

....
....
....
....
....
....
....
....
....
....
....
....

Love requires daily tending like a garden.

....
....
....
....
....
....
....
....
....
....
....
....

Open your heart to love, even when you're scared.

True love supports personal freedom.

Love flourishes in the soil of vulnerability.

Be the person you would want to be with.

A loving heart is a powerful healer.

....
....
....
....
....
....
....
....
....
....
....

Release perfectionism in your relationship—it has no place in love.

....
....
....
....
....
....
....
....
....
....
....

Be fully present when you're with your partner.

Trust the timing of your love journey.

Cherish the love that comes from within.

Loyalty and love go hand in hand.

Create a relationship where both partners feel safe to express themselves.

Sometimes, love is simply holding space for one another.

Love doesn't demand; it invites.

Every act of kindness strengthens the bond of love.

Prioritise emotional connection over perfection.

Speak your truth with love, not with blame.

This exercise is designed to promote deeper self-awareness, improve your relationship dynamics, and incorporate feng shui principles that support love and harmony in your home, offer a path to a more fulfilling and harmonious life.

Exercise 4: Enhancing Communication

Question: How can I improve communication in my relationships, and where do I feel misunderstood?

Action: Write a letter to yourself or your partner about an issue you've struggled to communicate. Don't hold back; express your feelings honestly. For feng shui, place a lapis lazuli crystal in your home (preferably in the Southwest corner) to enhance communication and understanding in your relationship.

Healing within leads to healthier relationships outside.

....
....
....
....
....
....
....
....
....
....

Love grows where compassion is nurtured.

....
....
....
....
....
....
....
....
....
....

In relationships, honesty builds intimacy.

Cherish the love you give as much as the love you receive.

Embrace the journey of love with patience.

A relationship built on trust can weather any storm.

Allow love to flow naturally without forcing it.

_____
_____
_____
_____
_____
_____
_____
_____
_____
_____
_____

Your partner is your teammate, not your opponent.

_____
_____
_____
_____
_____
_____
_____
_____
_____
_____
_____

Celebrate the uniqueness of your love story.

Listening is the first act of love.

Allow yourself to be loved as deeply as you love others.

Release the need to control your partner's journey.

Celebrate the beauty in your differences.

The best love is the love that allows you to be fully yourself.

In love, every moment together is a gift.

True love celebrates; it does not compete.

Healing yourself heals your relationship.

The strongest love comes from being indeed seen and accepted.

Find joy in the present moment with your partner.

Your love for yourself reflects the love you give others.

Be each other's greatest cheerleaders, not critics.

Patience and understanding deepen love.

....
....
....
....
....
....
....
....
....
....
....
....
....
....
....

Cherish the little moments; they become significant memories.

....
....
....
....
....
....
....
....
....
....
....
....
....
....
....

Let love be your guide, not fear.

This exercise is designed to promote deeper self-awareness, improve your relationship dynamics, and incorporate feng shui principles that support love and harmony in your home, offer a path to a more fulfilling and harmonious life.

Exercise 5: Balancing Giving and Receiving

Question: Do I give and receive love equally, or do I tend to give more than I allow myself to receive?

Action: Take a few moments to reflect on the balance of giving and receiving in your relationship. Make a conscious effort to ask for what you need: affection, time, or support. As a feng shui action, create symmetry in your bedroom by ensuring balanced objects on each side of your bed—two matching lamps or candles, for example.

True love accepts the past and builds a future together.

....
....
....
....
....
....
....
....
....
....
....
....

Trust the process of growing together in love.

....
....
....
....
....
....
....
....
....
....
....
....

A healthy relationship is a dance between togetherness and individuality.

Love thrives in the space of freedom, not control.

Every moment of love is an opportunity for gratitude.

Kindness is the quiet force that strengthens love.

Speak your partner's love language fluently.

Be the love you wish to receive.

Appreciation turns the ordinary into the extraordinary in love.

Love doesn't fix us; it helps us grow.

Forgive often, and love more.

A relationship is a mirror—what you give is what you see.

Hold space for your partner's growth without judgment.

Be present, for that is where love lives.

The love you seek is already within you.

In love, choose understanding over assumptions.

....

True love supports your highest potential.

....

Focus on what is right in your relationship, not what is wrong.

Love is felt in the unspoken moments of connection.

Celebrate your love every day, not just on special occasions.

A good relationship is a safe place for both joy and vulnerability.

Healthy boundaries create space for a deeper connection.

Don't wait for a special occasion to say "I love you."

Gratitude is the seed from which love blooms.

This exercise is designed to promote deeper self-awareness, improve your relationship dynamics, and incorporate feng shui principles that support love and harmony in your home, offer a path to a more fulfilling and harmonious life.

Exercise 6: Releasing Past Hurts

Question: What past emotional wounds am I holding onto that prevent me from experiencing more profound love?

Action: Spend time journaling about any lingering pain from past relationships. Write a letter of forgiveness to yourself or someone who hurt you, and then safely burn or discard the letter to symbolise release. In feng shui, place sage or incense in your home and perform a cleansing ritual to clear any lingering negative energy associated with past relationships.

The best relationships are based on mutual respect.

....
....
....
....
....
....
....
....
....
....

Love allows you to be both strong and soft.

....
....
....
....
....
....
....
....
....
....

Love is a two-way street; give and receive equally.

Love is a two-way street; give and receive equally.

....
....
....
....
....
....
....
....
....
....
....
....
....
....

The energy of love multiplies when shared freely.

....
....
....
....
....
....
....
....
....
....
....
....
....
....

See your partner with fresh eyes every day.

A relationship flourishes when both partners are free to grow.

The language of love is spoken through actions.

True love is when two people give without keeping a score.

You cannot pour from an empty cup—fill yourself with love first.

....
....
....
....
....
....
....
....
....
....
....
....
....
....
....

Honour the love you feel for yourself, and others will follow.

....
....
....
....
....
....
....
....
....
....
....
....
....
....
....

Love yourself as much as you love your partner.

Genuine connection happens when we listen without judgment.

....
....
....
....
....
....
....
....
....
....

Shared experiences and memories strengthen a relationship.

....
....
....
....
....
....
....
....
....
....

Love is an infinite resource—there's always more to give.

Release the need to change your partner—love them as they are.

....
....
....
....
....
....
....
....
....
....
....
....
....
....

Practice forgiveness, even when it's hard.

....
....
....
....
....
....
....
....
....
....
....
....
....
....

True love understands and respects differences.

Be patient; love requires time to grow.

....
....
....
....
....
....
....
....
....
....
....
....

Speak with kindness, especially during challenging moments.

....
....
....
....
....
....
....
....
....
....
....
....

Love is most powerful when it is patient and understanding.

Make time for love—it thrives in presence, not in a hurry.

Celebrate the love that exists today, not the love you wish for tomorrow.

Your relationship is a reflection of your inner world.

This exercise is designed to promote deeper self-awareness, improve your relationship dynamics, and incorporate feng shui principles that support love and harmony in your home, offer a path to a more fulfilling and harmonious life.

Exercise 7: Creating a Love Vision Board

Question: What do I genuinely want from love, and how can I align myself with this vision?

Action: Create a vision board with images, affirmations, and symbols representing your ideal love life. Place the board prominently in your home, such as in your bedroom or the southwest corner. This will be a visual reminder of the love you want to cultivate.

Let go of past disappointments and welcome new possibilities in love.

The most robust relationships are built on emotional safety.

Love is the bridge that connects hearts.

Let your partner know they are loved every single day.

....

....

....

....

....

....

....

....

....

....

....

....

....

....

Create space for love by releasing fear and doubt.

....

....

....

....

....

....

....

....

....

....

....

....

....

....

Be love in every interaction, and love will return to you.

Love is not about finding the perfect person but growing together.

The most profound love comes when we love without conditions.

True love doesn't control—it liberates.

The greatest gift you can give is your presence.

Love is felt in the smallest gestures.

The foundation of love is built on trust and vulnerability.

Let love guide your actions, even when you're hurt.

....
....
....
....
....
....
....
....
....
....
....

Show up fully in your relationship without holding back.

....
....
....
....
....
....
....
....
....
....
....

Let go of what no longer serves your relationship.

When you choose love over fear, you invite peace.

....
....
....
....
....
....
....
....
....
....
....
....
....
....

Love is the highest expression of your true self.

....
....
....
....
....
....
....
....
....
....
....
....
....
....

Be generous with your love—it only grows when shared.

Your partner's strengths are a gift—celebrate them.

....

....

....

....

....

....

....

....

....

....

....

A relationship is a partnership, not a competition.

....

....

....

....

....

....

....

....

....

....

....

....

Express your appreciation as often as possible.

Love is a commitment to seeing the best in each other.

Your love story is uniquely yours—embrace it.

Be open to receiving love in unexpected ways.

This exercise is designed to promote deeper self-awareness, improve your relationship dynamics, and incorporate feng shui principles that support love and harmony in your home, offer a path to a more fulfilling and harmonious life.

Exercise 8: Strengthening Trust

Question: How can I build trust in my relationship, and where must I let go of control?

Action: Reflect on areas of your relationship where trust has been challenged. Write down one way to actively build trust with your partner, whether through vulnerability or open communication. In feng shui, place amethyst or citrine crystals in your bedroom or living space to enhance emotional clarity and trust.

A relationship grows when both partners feel valued and respected.

Forgive yourself for past relationship mistakes—they were lessons.

Love grows deeper through patience and understanding.

True love is steady, not rushed.

Let love be your guiding force in all things.

In love, practice mindfulness and presence.

Every relationship offers an opportunity for growth and healing.

The best relationships are grounded in mutual respect.

Love with your whole heart, even when it feels vulnerable.

Cherish the moments when love feels easy.

....

Love doesn't compete; it complements.

....

Be present in your love, not just a participant.

Trust that love will always guide you home.

A loving relationship is a safe space for growth.

The more you love yourself, the deeper your capacity to love others.

Celebrate the journey of love, not just the destination.

Love is an action, not just a feeling.

Love creates space for healing and transformation.

Release fear, and love will fill its place.

Trust is the foundation upon which love grows.

Love is not about winning but about understanding.

Give love room to breathe and evolve.

In love, be open to receiving as much as giving.

Create a relationship that feels like a sanctuary.

This exercise is designed to promote deeper self-awareness, improve your relationship dynamics, and incorporate feng shui principles that support love and harmony in your home, offer a path to a more fulfilling and harmonious life.

Exercise 9: Honoring Intimacy and Vulnerability

Question: How comfortable am I with being vulnerable in love, and what fears hold me back from deeper intimacy?

Action: Choose a vulnerable truth about yourself that you've been afraid to share with your partner. Reflect on how sharing it could bring you closer. For feng shui, introduce soft textures and lighting into your bedroom to create an intimate, nurturing environment. Use warm colours like pink and peach to promote emotional openness.

Love starts with acceptance of yourself and others.

Let love be the reason for your actions, not fear.

The greatest love is the love that allows you to be free.

A relationship thrives when both partners choose kindness daily.

....
....
....
....
....
....
....
....
....
....
....
....
....

Be intentional about the love you give and receive.

....
....
....
....
....
....
....
....
....
....
....
....
....

True love enhances; it doesn't diminish.

In love, always choose understanding over anger.

....
....
....
....
....
....
....
....
....
....
....
....

Be your partner's most significant source of peace and comfort.

....
....
....
....
....
....
....
....
....
....
....
....

Love is built on the small, everyday acts of care.

Celebrate the unique love that you and your partner share.

Love grows when both partners feel appreciated and valued.

Trust the process of love—it unfolds in its own time.

Your relationship is a reflection of the love you give yourself.

....
....
....
....
....
....
....
....
....
....
....

Embrace the imperfections in love—they make it real.

....
....
....
....
....
....
....
....
....
....
....

Create space in your heart for love to grow.

Love is more powerful than any obstacle.

Be a source of light and love for your partner.

Love is the thread that connects all hearts.

Show gratitude for the love you already have.

_____
_____
_____
_____
_____
_____
_____
_____
_____
_____

Listen to your partner with an open heart and mind.

_____
_____
_____
_____
_____
_____
_____
_____
_____
_____

Choose love over judgment every time.

Celebrate the beauty of a love that grows through change.

Let go of old hurts and invite new love into your life.

Love is a journey of continuous growth and discovery.

This exercise is designed to promote deeper self-awareness, improve your relationship dynamics, and incorporate feng shui principles that support love and harmony in your home, offer a path to a more fulfilling and harmonious life.

Exercise 10: Clearing Emotional and Physical Space

Question: Is there any emotional or physical clutter in my life that blocks the flow of love and intimacy?

Action: Identify one physical space and one emotional area that needs clearing. Declutter a drawer, closet, or room, and then meditate on any lingering emotional baggage. In feng shui, burn sage or use a bell to clear stagnant energy in your home, paying particular attention to the bedroom and Southwest corner.

Be the love you want to see in your relationship.

Nurture your relationship like a precious garden.

Love allows us to see the world through another's eyes.

A loving relationship is one where both partners feel seen and heard.

Be fully present with your partner—it's the greatest gift you can give.

Love thrives on openness, trust, and vulnerability.

Choose to love, even when it's complicated.

The love you share today shapes your relationship tomorrow.

Every relationship teaches us something about ourselves.

Love flourishes when both partners feel supported and understood.

Celebrate the moments of connection that make love unique.

True love is grounded in patience, kindness, and trust.

Allow love to guide you, even through the challenges.

Forgiveness is the doorway to more profound love.

Nurture your relationship by giving it time, attention, and care.

Love is the most potent force in the universe.

The key to lasting love is consistency and compassion.

Embrace love with an open heart and mind.

True love grows in an environment of honesty and trust.

In love, always seek to understand before being understood.

Love creates the space for healing and renewal.

Celebrate your partner's uniqueness—it's what makes them unique.

Healthy love allows both partners to shine.

Appreciation turns simple moments into lasting memories.

This exercise is designed to promote deeper self-awareness, improve your relationship dynamics, and incorporate feng shui principles that support love and harmony in your home, offer a path to a more fulfilling and harmonious life.

Exercise 11: Setting Relationship Goals

Question: What are my goals for love and relationships, and how can I align my actions with these goals?

Action: Write down three specific goals for your love life, whether single or in a relationship. Take one tangible action toward each goal in the coming week. Enhance your bedroom or Southwest corner with paired objects or romantic symbols to reinforce these intentions.

Every day is an opportunity to strengthen your love.

....
....
....
....
....
....
....
....
....
....
....
....

A relationship is a dance between giving and receiving.

....
....
....
....
....
....
....
....
....
....
....
....

Love yourself enough to set healthy boundaries.

Be present in the love you have today, not just the love you want tomorrow.

True love lifts you; it never pulls you down.

Celebrate the love that grows through shared experiences.

Choose love in every decision you make.

Forgive yourself and your partner—it's the pathway to more profound love.

Love grows when both partners feel safe to be themselves.

True love supports both freedom and connection.

In love, every moment is a chance to deepen your bond.

Cherish the love that grows through change.

Be willing to grow together, not apart.

Love flourishes when we are kind to ourselves and others.

Create a space in your heart for love to grow.

Celebrate love in all its forms—big and small.

Love thrives on mutual respect and trust.

Be patient with love—it unfolds in its own time.

In love, always choose kindness over criticism.

True love is about supporting each other's dreams.

Let love be the driving force in your relationship.

The best relationships are rooted in mutual respect and understanding.

In love, it's the little things that matter the most.

Celebrate your partner's growth and evolution.

This exercise is designed to promote deeper self-awareness, improve your relationship dynamics, and incorporate feng shui principles that support love and harmony in your home, offer a path to a more fulfilling and harmonious life.

Exercise 12: Embracing Gratitude

Question: How often do I express gratitude for my partner, my relationship, and the love I have in my life?

Action: Write a gratitude list focusing on your relationship, your partner (or your desire for a future partner), and what you generally appreciate about love. Commit to sharing one item from this list with your partner or reflecting on it daily. In feng shui, enhance the Southwest corner with items symbolising joy and gratitude, such as bright flowers, candles, or artwork.

trip w...
in the mor...
nt out to some ...
of hours. Then we back ...
waterfall. At the waterfall,
for 30 mins. When we arrived ...
of the waterfall! The water was ...
crowded at all. I feel really good a...
We hung out there for about an hour ...

Love is most powerful when it is patient and kind.

Let go of control and trust the process of love.

In love, both partners need room to breathe and grow.

Love grows when we choose compassion over judgment.

Be grateful for the love you have, and more will flow your way.

A relationship flourishes when both partners feel heard.

Love gives without asking for anything in return.

....
....
....
....
....
....
....
....
....
....
....

True love is patient, kind, and unwavering.

....
....
....
....
....
....
....
....
....
....
....

Celebrate the love that surrounds you every day.

The love you give is the love you will receive.

....
....
....
....
....
....
....
....
....
....
....
....
....

Be kind to yourself—it's the foundation for healthy love.

....
....
....
....
....
....
....
....
....
....
....
....
....

Genuine love creates a space for both partners to thrive.

Love is an action that requires daily practice.

....
....
....
....
....
....
....
....
....
....
....
....

In love, patience and understanding go hand in hand.

....
....
....
....
....
....
....
....
....
....
....
....
....

Celebrate the moments that make your love story unique.

Healthy love allows both partners to grow independently and together.

....
....
....
....
....
....
....
....
....
....
....
....
....
....

Trust that love will always find a way.

....
....
....
....
....
....
....
....
....
....
....
....
....
....

Forgiveness strengthens the bond of love.

Love is most powerful when it is unconditional.

Appreciate the love you have while striving for more.

True love is about acceptance, not perfection.

A loving heart is always open to growth.

Trust the timing of love—it knows when to arrive.

Healthy love creates a foundation for growth and happiness.

This exercise promotes deeper self-awareness, improves relationship dynamics, and incorporates feng shui principles that support love and harmony in your home. Following this exercise can pave the way to a more fulfilling and harmonious life.

Exercise 13: The Purpose of Cultivating Self-Compassion

Question: How can I be kinder to myself when I face challenges or make mistakes?

Action: Spend 10 minutes journaling about a recent challenge in which you were hard on yourself. Write down how you would comfort a friend in the same situation and then offer that same kindness to yourself. This act of self-kindness can make you feel cared for and nurtured. To enhance self-compassion with feng shui, a practice that uses energy forces to harmonise individuals with their surrounding environment, place a soothing item like a lavender candle or soft cushion in the Southwest corner of your home. This placement is believed to symbolise gentleness and self-care, thereby reinforcing your self-compassion.

Love allows us to see the beauty in every moment.

....

....

....

....

....

....

....

....

....

....

....

Cherish the love you have, and it will continue to grow.

....

....

....

....

....

....

....

....

....

....

....

Healthy love is about creating space for growth and connection.

True love gives without expectation.

In love, always choose compassion over criticism.

Let your love story unfold naturally without forcing it.

Every moment of love is an opportunity to grow.

....
....
....
....
....
....
....
....
....
....
....
....

Love is the most potent force for change.

....
....
....
....
....
....
....
....
....
....
....
....

Celebrate the love that allows you to be fully yourself.

Healthy love creates room for vulnerability and honesty.

....
....
....
....
....
....
....
....
....
....
....
....
....

Let go of fear, and love will fill the space.

....
....
....
....
....
....
....
....
....
....
....
....
....
....

In love, it's the small moments that make the most significant difference.

Cherish the love that grows with time and experience.

Trust that love will guide you through life's challenges.

A relationship grows when both partners feel supported.

Celebrate the unique journey of your love story.

....
....
....
....
....
....
....
....
....
....
....
....
....
....

Healthy love allows for both freedom and commitment.

....
....
....
....
....
....
....
....
....
....
....
....
....
....
....

True love is patient and willing to wait.

True love requires both giving and receiving equally.

....
....
....
....
....
....
....
....
....
....

Celebrate the love that grows through shared experiences.

....
....
....
....
....
....
....
....
....
....
....
....

In love, always choose understanding over judgment.

Be the love you wish to receive.

Healthy love allows both partners to feel safe and valued.

Celebrate the love that grows through kindness and respect.

Engaging in this exercise can foster deeper self-awareness, improve relationship dynamics, and incorporate feng shui principles that support love and harmony in your home. Ultimately, it offers a path to a more fulfilling and harmonious life.

Exercise 14: Visualising Abundance in Love

Question: How can I invite a greater sense of love and abundance into my life?

Action: Close your eyes and spend five minutes visualising what an abundant, love-filled life looks like for you. This powerful act of visualisation can instil a sense of hope and anticipation. How do you feel, and what actions are you taking to cultivate this abundance? Write down your thoughts and feelings afterwards. In feng shui, add a wealth bowl or golden object to your living space or Southwest corner to symbolise attracting love and abundance into your life.

Cherish the love that you give and the love that you receive.

Trust the journey of love—it knows the way.

Healthy love is grounded in trust, respect, and communication.

In love, trust is the foundation for a lasting connection.

Let your love be a source of inspiration and strength.

Healthy love allows both partners to shine.

Celebrate the love that grows through mutual understanding.

In love, patience and trust go hand in hand.

Cherish the love you have—it's the foundation for everything else.

Healthy love is grounded in mutual respect and communication.

Celebrate the love that grows through shared moments and experiences.

In love, choose kindness over criticism.

Healthy love allows both partners to feel seen and heard.

....
....
....
....
....
....
....
....
....
....
....
....

Trust that love will always guide you in the right direction.

....
....
....
....
....
....
....
....
....
....
....
....

Celebrate the love that helps you to grow and evolve.

In love, trust and vulnerability are the keys to a lasting connection.

Celebrate the love that grows through patience and understanding.

In love, always choose compassion and kindness.

Cherish the love that grows through shared experiences and memories.

Celebrate the love you have today, and it will continue to grow tomorrow.

Love grows when both partners are willing to listen and learn.

Celebrate the love that grows through challenges.

Be present in your love—it's the greatest gift you can give.

By practising this exercise, you can cultivate a deeper self-awareness, improve your relationship dynamics, and incorporate feng shui principles that support love and harmony in your home. This, in turn, can lead to a more fulfilling and harmonious life.

Exercise 15: Embodying Confidence in Love

Question: How do I show up confidently in love and relationships, and where can I grow in self-assurance?

Action: Write about when you felt confident and empowered in love. Reflect on what helped you feel that way and how you can bring that confidence into your current or future relationships. As a feng shui action, introduce red into your bedroom or Southwest corner through pillows, art, or candles to symbolise passion, confidence, and strength in love.

Celebrate the love that will enable you to grow and evolve.

....
....
....
....
....
....
....
....
....
....

Love is most powerful when it is kind and patient.

....
....
....
....
....
....
....
....
....
....

Be present in your love, and it will continue to flourish.

It's okay to ask for what you need in love.

Every relationship is a reflection of self-love.

Kindness fuels the fire of love.

LOVE JOURNEY CHECKLIST

Use this flexible checklist to review your progress and ensure you incorporate love into your daily life. Mark each item as you complete it, and feel empowered to revisit any exercises that need more attention. This checklist is a tool for your journey, not a rigid set of rules.

Daily Practices:

- I take time each day to acknowledge and celebrate something I love about myself.
- I practice self-compassion, especially when I face challenges or make mistakes.
- I set healthy boundaries that protect my emotional and physical well-being.
- I regularly engage in activities that nourish my body, mind, and soul.
- I declutter my physical space to create room for love and harmony.

Weekly Actions:

- I reflect on my relationship patterns and consciously try to create positive change.
- I practice gratitude for the love I give and receive, both from myself and others.
- I set aside time for personal reflection and growth, focusing on nurturing my relationship with myself.
- I balance giving and receiving love in all my relationships.
- I enhance my living space using feng shui principles, paying attention to the Southwest corner to attract love and balance.

Monthly Check-In:

- I review my love journey and assess areas where I can improve.
- I declutter one area of my home that feels stagnant or heavy.
- I revisit a past emotional wound and reflect on how much healing I have achieved.
- I celebrate my progress and reward myself for my cultivated love.

Feng Shui Enhancements:

- My Southwest corner is clutter-free and contains symbols of love, balance, and self-compassion.
- I incorporate items that promote communication, harmony, and trust in my relationships (such as candles, crystals, or affirmations).
- My bedroom is a space of balance, with paired objects and soothing, warm colours to foster love and intimacy.

Love Goal Setting

As you conclude your love journey, set a tangible goal for the coming weeks or months. Write down one specific goal that reflects your commitment to continuing your growth in love.

My Love Goal:

"I commit to (insert your goal here) and will take daily/weekly/monthly actions to ensure I maintain and nurture my self-love. I understand that my relationship with myself is the foundation for all other relationships in my life."

Final Statement and Call to Action

By completing this checklist and setting your love goal, you affirm your commitment to nurturing a deeper, more compassionate relationship with yourself that invites lasting transformation in your personal life and relationships. Michele believes that the foundation of any healthy, loving relationship starts with self-value. Honouring your worth—your opinions, views, and actions—creates a space for others to love and value you equally.

Good luck on your incredible journey toward a future filled with love and limitless possibilities! To further enhance your understanding of how your home and relationships are intertwined, read *Beginner's Feng Shui: Love and Relationships*. This guide will support you in aligning your space with your relationship goals and cultivating a home filled with love, harmony, and happiness.

Michele xx

ABOUT THE AUTHOR

Michele has been in demand as a Feng Shui consultant for over two decades. She has been trained by Master Raymond Lo (from Hong Kong) and Juliana Abraham (from the Feng Shui Centre in Perth, Western Australia) and has studied with Dato Joey Yap and Lillian Too. Michele maintains her studies each year to ensure she continues to provide clients with the best of her skills. Michele has an uncanny ability to read charts and fantastic insight into people. She combines experience and natural intuition with the multi-layered discipline of Feng Shui to deliver positive client outcomes. Michele's approach is practical, realistic and straightforward. She adores the reward of making a difference in the lives of her valued clients.

Having studied architectural drafting and interior design and working with interiors and renovations on her own homes, it was a natural progression to incorporate Feng Shui and metaphysical studies into those projects. Applauded for her style, Michele was often asked if she could share her gift with others.

Passion and dedication, combined with further studies, saw her first Feng Shui business, Energise Life Feng Shui born and evolve into Complete Feng Shui.

Michele conducts onsite Feng Shui consultations for residential and corporate clients. An accredited teacher at recognised training institutes, author and public speaker with numerous radio and television guest appearances. Michele works alongside families with residential homes, developers, architects, interior designers, real estate agents, restaurants, cafes, day spas and retail stores.

For any existing or proposed business client Michele can help with staff recruitment, choosing the best location and orientation for business premises, improving the atmosphere and working environment, and advisement on business stationery such as letterheads and business cards.

For the residential client, Michele offers guidance on improving health and harmony in the home, choosing the best home for you and improving the chances of selling your home. Other services include how to select a suitable carer for children or elderly family members and how to improve children's behaviour, sleep and studies.

Michele's practice and qualifications include Classical, Form, 8 Mansions, 24 Mountain Compass, and Flying Star School Feng Shui. Site selection and design. Metaphysical studies of Four Pillars of Destiny / Bazi / Pa Chee, Qi Men, Millionaires Feng Shui with particular interest and studies on Feng Shui Love and relationship luck.

Michele teaches beginner to practitioner Feng Shui seminars, workshops, courses and retreats and conducts onsite learning experiences at homes and businesses. Students receive complete course notes. There are courses to explore for those who have mastered the basics of Feng Shui and wish to continue their studies and share their knowledge.

With an ability to relate to people from all walks of life. Based in Perth, but regularly consulting in Singapore, Bali and eastern states of Australia on residential, business, and commercial properties.

Michele truly believes:

"Life is what our thoughts, environment and energy make it". "Change your environment and thoughts; change your life".

With knowledge of Feng Shui, it can work to increase wealth, enhance health, and harmonise relationships.

Transform and Empower Your Love Life: A Love Reset Retreat in Bali-A Unique Opportunity to Reset Your Love Life

Ready to attract the relationship you've always dreamed of? Join Feng Shui Love specialist Michele Castle for an extraordinary retreat in Bali to help you transform your love life by aligning your mind, body, and surroundings. Dive into six days of indulgence and self-discovery in a traditional Balinese resort, where you'll learn how to unlock the secrets to lasting love and relationship harmony and discover more about yourself than you ever thought possible.

What Awaits You:
- **6 Days of Bliss:** Shop, relax, enjoy cocktails, and savour delicious cuisine as you soak in the beauty of Bali.
- **Authentic Chinese Bazi Love Profiling:** Discover your unique love potential and fast-track your future possibilities.
- **Enhance Relationship Harmony:** Learn Feng Shui principles to improve love and relationships.
- **Vibrate with Love & Abundance:** Tap into your unique energy to attract love and prosperity.
- **Indulge in a Spa Package:** Enjoy a 2-hour footbath, reflexology, massage, and body scrub.
- **Create Your Signature Scent:** Participate in a French Perfume workshop.
- **Culinary Adventure:** Take part in a traditional Indonesian cooking class.
- **Healing & Meditation:** Experience a healing day ceremony, water purification, meditation, and more.
- **Cultural Exploration:** Discover Ubud's rich culture, vibrant markets, and exquisite dining.
- **Sound Healing at the Pyramids of Chi:** Immerse yourself in a divine sound healing session.
- **Jewellery-Making Workshop:** Unleash your creativity in a fun and unique setting.
- **Luxury Accommodation:** Stay at a boutique-style hotel, with breakfast, teas, and airport transfers included.

Rejuvenate your soul and reconnect with what makes you unique. This retreat allows you to reset your love life and embrace the love you deserve.

Visit https://completelifestyleretreat.com.au/ or https://www.facebook.com/completelifestyleretreats to explore past retreats.

Take this time for yourself. Your love life is waiting to be transformed!

HAVE YOU ENJOYED BEGINNERS FENG SHUI LOVE AND RELATIONSHIPS?

Introducing Michele Castle's groundbreaking first book in the Beginner's Feng Shui Trilogy: Beginners Feng Shui, Easy Tips to Enhance Everyday Living, The Art of Placement and Manipulation of Energy. This indispensable guide, born from Michele's twenty years of expertise, is a comprehensive step-by-step manual. It's tailored for those seeking to unleash their home's full potential, offering practical strategies deeply rooted in the ancient principles of Feng Shui. These strategies, unique to this book, enable you to easily enhance your health, wealth, relationships, or career.

By delving into symbolism, placement, and colour, Michele imparts invaluable insights that are both easy to apply and transformative. This book is not just a guide; it's a compelling call to join the Feng Shui revolution and revolutionize your world from the core.

Praise for Beginners Feng Shui: "A must-read! Be empowered with these easy tips to enhance your everyday life. I highly recommend you harness the Feng Shui expertise of Michele Castle to live your best, abundant life and maximise your positive energy to sustain a happy life and an overall sense of well-being." – Margie Bryant, Life by Design.

"My life has positively transformed after reading, adjusting, and following Michele's knowledge. I am deeply grateful and will recommend this book gem to my clients." – Odette Linton.

Beginners Feng Shui www.completefengshui.com

PERIOD 9 IN FENG SHUI AND CHINESE ASTROLOGY

Explore the potential of Period 9 in Feng Shui and Chinese Astrology from 2024 to 2044. Discover the captivating influence of this twenty-year cycle starting on February 4, 2024. Unleash the power of the Fire Element during Period 9, igniting personal growth, creativity, and innovation. This period offers limitless opportunities and transformation. Learn tailored Feng Shui techniques to align with Period 9's energies, manifesting dreams into reality. Dive into the journey, transforming living or workspaces into vibrant sanctuaries. Stay in sync with cosmic forces using flying stars and dynamic period energy. Join a community of seekers on this life-changing path of growth and prosperity guided by Chinese metaphysics. Embrace Period 9's electrifying power for a transformative journey into a future full of possibilities, altering the trajectory of your life.

Period 9 in Feng Shui and Chinese Astrology www.completefengshui.com

www.ingramcontent.com/pod-product-compliance
Lightning Source LLC
Chambersburg PA
CBHW051437290426
44109CB00016B/1590